PARTIAL OBJECTS

a fairy tale about what
happens in the night

Sherry Kramer

BROADWAY PLAY PUBLISHING INC
224 E 62nd St, NY, NY 10065
www.broadwayplaypub.com
info@broadwayplaypub.com

First printing: December 2011
I S B N: 978-0-88145-519-9

Book design: Marie Donovan
Page make-up: Adobe Indesign
Typeface: Palatino
Printed and bound in the U S A

PARTIAL OBJECTS premiered in 1993 at Mill Mountain Theater (Executive and Artistic Director, Jere Lee Hodgin) in Roanoke, Virginia as part of The Norfolk Southern Festival of New Works. The cast and creative contributors were:

MEPHISTOPHELES .... Adrian Williams
PARIS .... Jerry Bradley
JULIANNA ....Martha Perantoni
MARGARET .... Wendy A Rolfe

Director .... Ernest Zulia
Stage manager ....Cindi Raebel
Dramaturge .... Jo Weinstein
Costume designer .... Anne Toewe
Scenery & lighting ....John Sailer

CHARACTERS & SETTING

MEPHISTOPHELES, *played by an actor who, if he had been smaller, would have played Puck, when he was younger; but it is now exactly just too late.*

PARIS, *played by a charming, likable actor, mid to late thirties; he'll look like a boy all his life.*

JULIANNA, *played by an actress who has been cast in comedic parts one time too many; early thirties.*

MARGARET, *played by an actress who can play from six years old to thirty years old*

Setting: PARIS'*s and* JULIANNA'*s apartments, and a few places in between*

Time: The present

Music: A score should be designed to accompany MEPHISTOPHELES *at beginning and end of* ACT ONE, *and elsewhere when appropriate.*

for David Juaire

ACT ONE

PROLOGUE—ON EARTH

(MEPHISTOPHELES *appears, wearing a black cloak lined with blood red, and walking with a slight limp. He carries a cane with a silver poodle handle.*)

(*He performs a few simple card tricks for the benefit of the audience. These need be no more complicated than any that a child could do—the important issue is that they are done with style, panache, showmanship.*)

(*He sets up two hands of cards on a small table down stage— then checks both hands and, considering for an instant, plucks an ace from the deck and tucks it in his sleeve. He turns to go, then turns back, addressing the audience.*)

MEPHISTOPHELES: Well, come on, now—you don't expect me to insult you by pretending to have nothing up my sleeve, do you?
No, that fits right in with your ideas about me. In fact, you've been thinking and saying the most terrible things about me for the longest time.
Well, stop—

(MEPHISTOPHELES *makes a magical gesture. Great bolts of lightning crash, and thunder cracks loudly.*)

MEPHISTOPHELES: STOP!!!!!!

(*Lightning and thunder increase.*)

MEPHISTOPHELES: STOOOOOOOOOOP—

(The lightning and thunder cease abruptly as MEPHISTOPHELES *stops himself from further fury.)*

(He holds his head in his hands, gaining control.)

(After a moment, he looks up, smiling bravely.)

MEPHISTOPHELES: I'm better now. I'm all right. Don't worry, I don't want you going home tonight and saying "Oh, Lucifer himself had a nervous breakdown right on stage, it was soooooooooo booooooring. We half expected that at any minute he would regale us with stories about his much abused childhood. Z z z." I mean, who cares? Everybody had a rough childhood. Everybody had a father who didn't understand them. Everybody wants to take it out on everybody—but nobody but Satan worked out his adolescent anger by trying to destroy the world, did they?

No.

So go on, saying those terrible things about me. Go on—believe the world itself is running away in these arms. *(He raises his arms out in front of him.)* You say my arms are strong enough to carry you away from what makes the birds sing and the heart rejoice. But you know nothing about these arms. *(He lowers his arms.)*

Listen—you and I—we're not so very different. You and I—we're really quite alike. We both dream the same dream, we both long to be reunited with a piece of ourselves we've lost, we long with the same ache to return to the safe place, we dream of feeling God's grace once again! *(He sees that we don't believe him.)* You don't believe me. Nevertheless it's true. Everything I've ever done, I've done for one reason only—to get home. That's what I'm doing here, on earth. Trying to get all of us home. Home. Ah, yes. I remember, it's your curse to see heaven heavy with angels, beating their wings, lazy in the radiance of the vague, pure, everlasting.

And it's mine, and all the angels' curse to curse you for the blindness that sees us there. An angel may not love, and suffering finds us everywhere we search for the one, true heaven, which is here— *(He indicates the audience.)* —here, in this heroic landscape, this maze of redemption, this—

(Lights up on a bed.)

MEPHISTOPHELES: —small place of impassioned astronomy. *(He walks over to the bed, sits down on it.)* This place, where two bodies and two souls in perfect desire resemble God's face, on the face of the earth. You know what I'm talking about. Don't pretend you don't, you know you do. You know you were born to feel heaven in a touch. To understand the secrets of the universe in the way the breathing of the person sleeping beside you fills the lost night air. You know you were born to feel something—magnificent. *(He gets up, walks down stage, leaving the bed behind in a pool of light.)*

Wouldn't you give anything to feel that magnificent something? To feel the sweet warm slash of redemption? Would you give your soul to feel it? Would you? What if someone walked up to you, right now, and said that if you gave your soul, you'd feel what you can just remember so deep inside you, you could pull yourself apart with knives and never find it— *(Intimate, really intimate with the audience, truly excited)* —if someone said, just give your soul, and you will feel that place—yes—that—the place where dim recall past knowing sees a face of beauty past belief— *(He almost sees it.)* —you'd give it. *(He makes a magical gesture.)*

(Blackout)

Scene One

(*Beat 1: Fireworks appear inside* PARIS*'s bedroom. Gradually they illuminate the room, revealing* PARIS, *standing on his bed. He throws his arms in the air, laughing.*)

PARIS: Do it again! Do it again!

(*More explosions of lovely, red and gold light.* PARIS *dances in the light.*)

(*Blackout*)

(*Beat 2*: PARIS *and* MEPHISTOPHELES *playing cards. A few cards are played.*)

PARIS: Gin. (*Laying down his cards.*)
You know what that means.

(*Blackout*)

(*Beat 3: * PARIS *and* MEPHISTOPHELES *suspended in the room, flying. They tilt and bank in tandem. The wind whips through their hair.*)

PARIS: Oh, look—there's the Effil Tower! Shit!!!! There's the Great Wall! Wow!
Hey, that forest down there. It looks like the Garden of—

(*Blackout*)

(*Beat 4*: PARIS *and* MEPHISTOPHELES *playing cards.* PARIS *is now wearing a shiny black visor. After a few cards are played:*)

PARIS: Guess what? (*He lays his cards down.*)

(*Blackout*)

(*Beat 5:* PARIS *runs in place, with one arm held up, holding a torch. He is out of breath. He stumbles, catches himself, goes on. The Olympic theme music blares out, and he "climbs" the stairs to the Olympic flame—which he lights, to thunderous applause.*)

(*Blackout*)

(*Beat 6:* PARIS *and* MEPHISTOPHELES *playing cards.* PARIS *is now wearing a riverboat gambler's hat. A few cards are played. It may be noticed that* PARIS *picks up every card* MEPHISTOPHELES *discards.*)

PARIS: You won't believe this, but— (*He puts down his cards.*) Gin.

(MEPHISTOPHELES *can't help smiling.*)

(*Blackout*)

(*Beat 7: A huge nuclear missile with prominent Iranian markings is in the room.* PARIS, *using a huge wrench, is messing around in the missile's mechanism. He pulls out an oversized computer chip, smashes part of it, replaces the chip and closes the door to the compartment.*)

PARIS: Okay. That takes care of all the dirty bombs headed in the direction of my parent's house.

(*Blackout*)

(*Beat 8:* MEPHISTOPHELES *and* PARIS *playing cards.* MEPHISTOPHELES *discards, face down.* PARIS *instinctively goes to pick it up—*MEPHISTOPHELES *puts one hand over* PARIS's, *and with the other lays down his hand—it's gin.*)

MEPHISTOPHELES: Gin.

PARIS: Oh. Well, I guess I couldn't keep up that streak forever. So. What do you want?

MEPHISTOPHELES: A kiss.

PARIS: What?

MEPHISTOPHELES: A kiss.

PARIS: A kiss? What do you mean, a kiss?

MEPHISTOPHELES: A kiss.

PARIS: But you're a man—I mean—I know you're not really a man, I mean you're not either, but—I mean I know we had a deal, but—

(Blackout)

*(**Beat 9**: MEPHISTOPHELES seated on the bed. He pats the place next to him. PARIS sits. MEPHISTOPHELES kisses PARIS. PARIS endures it bravely.)*

(Blackout)

*(**Beat 10**: MEPHISTOPHELES and PARIS playing cards. PARIS is obviously very nervous. PARIS is wiping his face, wringing his hands, fumbling with his cards. MEPHISTOPHELES wins.)*

MEPHISTOPHELES: Gin.

PARIS: Shit.

MEPHISTOPHELES: Another.

PARIS: Now listen here, I—

MEPHISTOPHELES: Another kiss.

(Blackout)

*(**Beat 11**: MEPHISTOPHELES and PARIS kiss. This time, PARIS kisses him back.)*

(Blackout)

(*Beat 12:* MEPHISTOPHELES *wins.* PARIS *throws his cards into the air.*)

(*Blackout*)

(*Beat 13:* MEPHISTOPHELES *and* PARIS *sleeping in each other's arms. A soft rose light fills the room.*)

(*Blackout*)

Scene Two

(*Just before dawn.* MEPHISTOPHELES *is floating above* PARIS' *bed, lying on his side with his head propped up on his elbow.*)

MEPHISTOPHELES: I don't know what all the fuss is all about. It's really very cut and dried.

PARIS: It's my soul. My soul!

MEPHISTOPHELES: Nonsense. Before I came you didn't think you had one.

PARIS: I don't see why you can't love me without it.

MEPHISTOPHELES: Who said anything about love?

PARIS: Let's go someplace, okay? Someplace where there aren't a lot of people. Morocco. Tahiti.

MEPHISTOPHELES: No more Morocco and no more Tahiti.

PARIS: Then how about my sister's house in Jersey? I haven't seen the new baby yet.

MEPHISTOPHELES: You really try my nerves. Why do you want to make me angry?

PARIS: I'm not the one who's trying to make anyone angry.

MEPHISTOPHELES: And I am?

PARIS: You have this thing about saying you love me.

MEPHISTOPHELES: It's not a thing about saying it. It's something I can't say.

PARIS: Yeah, yeah. Go ahead and hide behind an angel can't do this and that crap.

MEPHISTOPHELES: It is hardly crap.

PARIS: It is to me.

MEPHISTOPHELES: It wasn't last night.

PARIS: Stop talking to me about last night! I can't think about anything else! I've never been held like I was last night. What are you going to do about that! Tell me! What are you going to do about that!

MEPHISTOPHELES: I've already told you. Last night wasn't real.

PARIS: Don't do this to me!

MEPHISTOPHELES: Last night was an illusion.

PARIS: What are you talking about? The Great Wall, the Eiffel Tower, that—

MEPHISTOPHELES: All that you felt and all that you saw with me was mere illusion. You never left this room.

PARIS: But after, when you kissed me...

MEPHISTOPHELES: Apparition. Fantasy. Dream.

PARIS: I won't believe that!

MEPHISTOPHELES: Believe. I never touched you, or you me.

PARIS: You wanted me.

MEPHISTOPHELES: Someone had to hold your head down for you. Someone had to teach you how to pray.

PARIS: You liked it!

MEPHISTOPHELES: Liked it! I would love it, if I could. But you were made for love, not me.

PARIS: You're just a whore!

MEPHISTOPHELES: *(Bows, elegantly)* For God, and no one else.

PARIS: You go to hell!!!

MEPHISTOPHELES: Been there. Done that. Listen. The moment for which you promised your soul will not be with me.

PARIS: Why not?

MEPHISTOPHELES: It will be with a woman.

PARIS: Who said anything about a woman?

MEPHISTOPHELES: You did, actually.

PARIS: When!

MEPHISTOPHELES: Last night. In the heat of passion. You called out a beautiful name.

PARIS: But I can't have it with anyone but you. It's not something that happens here.

MEPHISTOPHELES: You seem to think it did.

PARIS: That's different. It was with you.

MEPHISTOPHELES: With this woman it will be real.

PARIS: But I want you!

MEPHISTOPHELES: You want what you had last night.

PARIS: And why shouldn't I?

MEPHISTOPHELES: With this woman you will not have to share an illusion. You will have something real.

PARIS: *(Laughing)* Real? You don't know the first thing about it. Last night was real.

MEPHISTOPHELES: With a woman, Paris, you can—

PARIS: Can what. WHAT! Look. Here's what happens
with a woman. Here's what you think is real.
I meet her. I wait for her to say she loves me. She says
it. I look at her. I say to myself: "The rest of my life.
Does this woman look like the rest of my life?" She
doesn't. Or, it happens like this.
I meet her. I wait for her to say she loves me. She
doesn't. I realize I have to be the one who says it. I say
it. Guess what happens next. Go on. Can't? After I say
I love you I get to watch her look at me and say, to
herself: "The rest of my life. Do I want this person to be
my life for the rest of my life?"
Last night was real.

MEPHISTOPHELES: Then one woman is like another to
you, and it doesn't matter who I bring?

PARIS: No matter who you bring me, it will end the
same.

MEPHISTOPHELES: You're sure?

PARIS: Are you asking me who I'd like? Because if you
are, I'll tell you.

MEPHISTOPHELES: Who?

PARIS: Marilyn Monroe.

MEPHISTOPHELES: *(A bit disgusted)* Sorry.

PARIS: Yeah, I'll bet.

MEPHISTOPHELES: I've someone else in mind for you.

PARIS: You do? Then why haven't you brought her
here!

MEPHISTOPHELES: I will.

PARIS: When?

MEPHISTOPHELES: Soon.

PARIS: Why not now?

MEPHISTOPHELES: I must first show her what I've shown you.

PARIS: Oh.

What do you mean...show her?

MEPHISTOPHELES: You know what I mean.

PARIS: Do you have to? I mean, isn't there some other way?

MEPHISTOPHELES: Not if she's to promise her soul.

PARIS: Well, what if she doesn't? What if she doesn't want to give you her soul?

MEPHISTOPHELES: You forget who you are talking to, Paris.

PARIS: Yeah, but if she doesn't want to I've given you my soul for nothing!

MEPHISTOPHELES: I will not take your soul until you've had the moment you've been promised.
The two of you, together.

PARIS: But what if we can't?

MEPHISTOPHELES: The risk is mine.

PARIS: You're going to her tonight?

MEPHISTOPHELES: I am. It is time for the dream to end.

(MEPHISTOPHELES *snaps his fingers.* PARIS *falls immediately asleep, standing up.*)

MEPHISTOPHELES: Sleep—and when you wake, say nothing of what has happened.

(PARIS, *sound asleep, backs into bed and lies down.*)

Sleep. (*Gathering himself up in his cloak for his dramatic exit.*)

The day breaks. The night dies. And the Prince of Darkness flies. (*He flies away.*)

(Blackout)

Scene Three

(A few hours later. JULIANNA *is sitting near the open door, wearing her coat and a look of incredible unbelief.)*

JULIANNA: Now wait a minute. Let me get this straight. I come over for breakfast, and just like that, it's over?

PARIS: I told you I can't explain it.

JULIANNA: I don't care what you can't. I came over here for breakfast, let's go. We'll go and come back and then we'll see.

PARIS: Julie—

JULIANNA: Breakfast is my favorite meal. It's good no matter where you go and it's the best meal deal for the money. Even MacDonalds makes a great breakfast. Their hash browns are too greasy but their hotcakes are good.
Come on. We're going to breakfast. And then we'll come back here and talk.

PARIS: Julianna, please, don't—

JULIANNA: Charlie's makes a great breakfast. They have those waffles that they're famous for. Everybody knows about their waffles. They make them to order for you, don't leave 'em sitting around. If they left 'em sitting around they'd get hard and stale and they wouldn't be famous for them. Let's go. Let's get some breakfast and then we'll talk.

PARIS: Listen to me, I can't talk about it, I can't, I—

JULIANNA: I could make you breakfast! We could stay and I could make you breakfast here! I could make the omelet, or you could. I could fry the bacon first and make the eggs, or you could wash the pan and

make them after. We could have rye toast if you have
it, or just make do with white. We could squeeze fresh
orange juice if you have juice oranges. We'll make
coffee and then we'll set the table and then sit down
together.

We'll have our orange juice and we'll have our toast
and we'll have our eggs and our bacon and after that
we'll have our coffee.

Or we'll have them all together.

And then we'll talk.

PARIS: All right, Julie. Enough.

JULIANNA: What do you mean, enough? It's not
enough. It was never enough, someone saying they
couldn't say why and it's not enough now and you
know it. So just say you don't love me, and let me go.

PARIS: I do love you, Julie, I just...

JULIANNA: Don't love me enough?

PARIS: Listen to me, didn't you ever have something
happen to you that didn't make sense, but made all the
sense in the world? Something that just ripped up your
life and you fell all in pieces? Something that—

JULIANNA: If you're talking to me about seeing some
woman's legs on the subway, you'd just better stop. I
don't want to her about another woman. I want to hear
about *you*, and *me*, and *you and me*.

PARIS: Look, maybe I'd better call you tomorrow.

JULIANNA: I don't want to hear it tomorrow, I want to
hear it now. I want to hear you say "I don't love you"
and then I'll go.

Come on, it's a phrase you've said a million times, but
this time, it's got a don't after the I, it's very simple.

Come on, Perry. Say it.

PARIS: No.

JULIANNA: Then I don't go home.

I don't go home and we spend the day together, sitting in this room, we spend the day and the night and all the days and nights after. Until you say it.
Look at me. Look at me please, and say it.

PARIS: *(Sighs)* Come on. Let's go have breakfast.

JULIANNA: HOW CAN YOU TALK TO ME ABOUT BREAKFAST! *(Realizes. Beat)*
SHIT.

PARIS: What are we gonna do?

JULIANNA: I don't know, I don't know.
I don't know.

PARIS: I don't know.

JULIANNA: You're supposed to know.

PARIS: I know.

JULIANNA: Just say it, Perry, one time, fast, or slow, or very quiet if it's easier. I love you and I'm asking you to say it once. Then I'll leave and it will be all right.
I won't stay in bed for three or four weeks crying out your name in a room with the shades drawn. I promise.
Say it and it will be all right. I love you enough to believe you.

PARIS: Do you.

JULIANNA: Yes.

PARIS: But not enough to leave unless I say it?

JULIANNA: You can't have it both ways, Perry.

PARIS

But I love you, Julie, I just—

JULIANNA: Don't love me enough to say it, once and for all, and let me go?

But I do. *(She kisses him.)*
I don't love you. *(She turns to go.)*

PARIS: Julianna, wait—

JULIANNA: No.

PARIS: But you don't understand—

JULIANNA: What is there to understand? You don't love me.

PARIS: I never said—

JULIANNA: Not enough. *(She leaves.)*

(Blackout)

Scene Four

(The middle of the night. JULIANNA's *apartment. She walks into her bedroom.* MEPHISTOPHELES *is lying on her bed.)*

JULIANNA: What, again? How do you get in here?

MEPHISTOPHELES: It's four o'clock in the morning. Where have you been?

JULIANNA: Where have I been? Where do you get off asking *me* where *I've* been? Last night I wake up, from a deep, untroubled sleep. You're bending over my bed. I don't scream. It's not the first time I've seen a dark shape bending over me in the dark. This is the first time it's real. It takes me awhile to realize that so I don't scream. I think about screaming. Before I know it you're in bed beside me. I decide that it's time to scream. I open my mouth and I scream. There's no sound.
This has happened to me before, but only in nightmares. I remember a painting I once saw of a woman dreaming about a hideous horse's head leering above her. I'd prefer the horse's head.

You start floating above me and I shut my eyes. When I open them later you're gone.

I get up this morning, take a shower and shave my legs. I wash my hair and do my nails. I go over to have breakfast with the only man I've ever really loved and he tells me it's over and he can't say why.

Now tell me who the hell you are and how you got in here.

MEPHISTOPHELES: He didn't tell you why?

JULIANNA: No.

MEPHISTOPHELES: I'm sorry.

JULIANNA: Yeah.

(JULIANNA *sits on the bed next to* MEPHISTOPHELES. *He puts his arm around her.*)

JULIANNA: So am I.

MEPHISTOPHELES: Through the window.

JULIANNA: What?

MEPHISTOPHELES: I came in through your bedroom window.

JULIANNA: Oh. Sure. Why not.

MEPHISTOPHELES: What do you mean, sure, why not. Your bedroom window is fourteen stories up.

JULIANNA: A man can change completely in one day, I figure pigs can fly.

MEPHISTOPHELES: What's that supposed to mean?

JULIANNA: That I'm living in a dream world. And you're just part of the dream.

(MEPHISTOPHELES *begins to kiss* JULIANNA's *neck. He continues to caress and kiss her throughout her speech.*)

JULIANNA: After I left him I wandered the streets. It's what they do in movies, and I had nothing better to do. Just wandering's not what it's cracked up to be, so I started following. I followed men. Any man at first, then younger ones who looked like if I followed them I'd find out why I shouldn't. I got on buses going crazy places. I got off at their stops and looked around for more. There aren't enough of them to really go around above ground so I went under. You make better time on the trains and that gives you an edge. Underground there's plenty to choose from. A lot of them walk like they know something. The way some of them walked told me stories I couldn't begin to repeat to you now. Then one story looked like the last and they all looked alike. I come home, and you're here, and I don't know why I'm not screaming.

MEPHISTOPHELES: Turn out the light, Julianna.

JULIANNA: You know my name. That should surprise me. Nothing surprises me. I wish it did. Does that mean I'm getting old? I wonder.

MEPHISTOPHELES: It means I know your name.

JULIANNA: I don't know yours.

MEPHISTOPHELES: You will.

JULIANNA: Don't tell me yet. I'll put out the light. *(She stands, and puts out the lights.)*

(Blackout)

Scene Five

(Early morning. JULIANNA is dressed, making coffee and putting on her coat.)

JULIANNA: I don't know how you like it.

MEPHISTOPHELES: *(Stumbling out of bed)* What?

JULIANNA: Your coffee. Black? Regular? Just sugar? Cream?

MEPHISTOPHELES: What are you doing! You're leaving? Where are you going?

JULIANNA: Out. To the park or something. Walk around. Figure a few things out.

MEPHISTOPHELES: But what about me?

JULIANNA: Well, normally I'd ask you to leave when I did, but since you'll probably want to leave the way you came you'll have to find your own way out. Is that okay? I'm not being inhospitable? *(Pause)* What? You expected breakfast? What? Talk to me. Look. My life has just exploded in my face. Whoosh. You were very sweet last night, but if my plans don't jibe with yours that's just too bad. Maybe you like to go out for brunch after but I don't. In fact, there are certain things about you that would surprise me, I'm sure, if I saw you eat. You're quite an acrobat, you know that? You're something else. If things were different in my life I'm sure things between us would be...different. But they're not.
So. How do you like your coffee?

MEPHISTOPHELES: *(Speechless)* I—I—

JULIANNA: The sugar and cream are where you'd think they'd be, you can find everything yourself. The hot water takes along time in the morning, so if you take a shower, be prepared. The clean towels are easy to find, and use the Safeguard, not the pink soap, that's my face soap, if you don't mind.

MEPHISTOPHELES: But—

JULIANNA: It was nice, okay? Very nice. Really nice, okay? But I gotta get out of here. You make me a little crazy and I don't know what to think.

MEPHISTOPHELES: Julianna, wait—

JULIANNA: No. You make me a lot crazy. *(She rushes for the door. Opens it and goes out. Sticks her head back in.)* See you. *(And is gone.)*
(Blackout)

Scene Six

(PARIS' bedroom. MEPHISTOPHELES materializes in a burst of half-hearted red flame. PARIS is sitting, dejected, on the edge of his bed. They stare at each other for several moments.)

MEPHISTOPHELES: Miss me? *(No response)*
Paris? *(No response)*
Come on, Paris. Tell me how you missed me. Tell me how much.
Tell me—did you pace the floor? Bite your nails? Cry out my name?

PARIS: No. I didn't. I called my mother.

MEPHISTOPHELES: Hmmm. How is she?

PARIS: Fine. She said she was happy to hear the sound of my voice.

MEPHISTOPHELES: Yes, they always are, aren't they? God's a lot like that, you know.

PARIS: Like what.

MEPHISTOPHELES: Like your mother. Doesn't really care why He's hearing from you, just so long as He does.

PARIS: Are you going to stay with me tonight?

MEPHISTOPHELES: I'm sorry.

PARIS: If you're not going to stay with me then leave me alone.

MEPHISTOPHELES: You are alone.

PARIS: Then stay with me!

MEPHISTOPHELES: I have to go to her—

PARIS: Why is it taking so long!

MEPHISTOPHELES: She's in love.

PARIS: With you? Great. Just great.

MEPHISTOPHELES: Not with me. With a man she already knows—and frankly, what she sees in him I couldn't possibly guess.

PARIS: Great. Just how much longer is it going to take?

MEPHISTOPHELES: I don't know. I've never had this much trouble before.

PARIS: Oh, great, just great.

MEPHISTOPHELES: I've trotted out every trick I know and it hasn't worked.

PARIS: You must be doing something wrong.

MEPHISTOPHELES: Oh, you're a fine one to hand out advice when it comes to women.

PARIS: What's that supposed to mean!

MEPHISTOPHELES: And to think I came to you for help!

PARIS: I was doing fine—just fine until you showed up.

MEPHISTOPHELES: Oh, yes, fine, fine. Do you have any idea how hard it's going to be for me to go back there again tonight? Do you?

PARIS: Then stay with me. I missed you.

MEPHISTOPHELES: I cannot. *(He begins to disappear.)*

PARIS: What makes you think you'll have any better luck with her tonight!

MEPHISTOPHELES: *(As he vanishes)* Faith. Hope. And woman's basic charity. *(He is gone.)*

(Blackout)

Scene Seven

(JULIANNA *quietly opens the door to her apartment. Sneaks inside without turning on the light. Tiptoes into her bedroom, unaware that a large black poodle, wearing a studded red collar and walking with a slight limp has followed her inside. She flicks on the light switch.*)

JULIANNA: AHHH-HA!! (*But* MEPHISTOPHELES *is not there. She pauses, then bolts over to the floor length curtains, pulls them back.*) AH-HA! (*He's not there either. She throws herself on all fours and sticks her head under the bed.*) Ah-Ha? (*Not there either. She is puzzled, then leaps up and swings the closet door open.*) Ah-ha... (*No success. She looks around. There is no place left big enough to conceal a man, but she checks under the bedspread, behind the headboard, etc. Finally she plops down on the bed, defeated. The poodle trots over, and jumps up on the bed beside her.*) I can't believe this. You followed me all the way home? What are you doing on the bed? Your feet are dirty, there's no telling where you've been. Where ever that nose of yours tells you to go those feet of yours have to follow. Get down. Get.

(*The poodle jumps down, sits begging at* JULIANNA'*s feet.*)

JULIANNA: Good. That's very good. Now. Go home. You heard me, go. Go or I'll follow you. How would you like that? Strange woman following you home.

(*The poodle just sits.*)

JULIANNA: Okay. So you're staying. Just don't get on the bed.

(*The poodle whines. She sighs and turns to take off the bedspread.*)

JULIANNA: Okay. Go ahead.

(*The poodle transform into* MEPHISTOPHELES.)

JULIANNA: Very funny.

MEPHISTOPHELES: Glad you think so.

JULIANNA: Where's the dog?

MEPHISTOPHELES: The what?

JULIANNA: The poodle. Where've you got him?

MEPHISTOPHELES: He's gone.

JULIANNA: Look, I know how you guys work. You've got him hidden somewhere... *(She checks.)* You're really good, you know that? An acrobat and a magician. Do you juggle?

MEPHISTOPHELES: Do I juggle?

JULIANNA: My first boy friend could juggle.

MEPHISTOPHELES: No, I don't juggle.

JULIANNA: A shame. With your other talents you could put on quite an act.

MEPHISTOPHELES: A shame.

JULIANNA: I knew you'd come back.

MEPHISTOPHELES: Did you?

JULIANNA: I just didn't think it would be as a dog.

MEPHISTOPHELES: Well, I have to have my fun, don't I?

JULIANNA: I don't know. Do you?

MEPHISTOPHELES: Yes.

JULIANNA: Well, you've had it.
Look, the dog isn't in any pain or anything, is he? He's where he can get some air? Not too cramped.

MEPHISTOPHELES: He's fine.

JULIANNA: Okay, just checking. I got soft spot for dogs.

MEPHISTOPHELES: I was counting on that.

JULIANNA: There isn't any dog, is there?

MEPHISTOPHELES: No.

JULIANNA: That's what I was afraid of.

(MEPHISTOPHELES *pulls* JULIANNA *to him and kisses her. She pulls away.*)

JULIANNA: Please don't. Don't. You're gonna start and then I won't know who I am and there won't be anyone left to tell you to stop. So don't start.

MEPHISTOPHELES: I never force myself on anyone.

JULIANNA: Yeah, well, I'm not saying no, and I'm not saying maybe, I'm saying let's talk. I like to hear a man talk, you know? It gets me used to the sound of his voice so I know who's talking if he calls out a name in the heat of passion that's not mine.

MEPHISTOPHELES: All right. What would you like me to talk about?

JULIANNA: I like a man to talk about himself. You find out, right away, just how far gone he is. Men can fool you if they talk about things they know about, like art or real estate or public T V. They fool you the worst if they talk about their fathers. I like them to talk about themselves. Then you can see right through them because who they say they are, and who they look like to you are two entirely different things. Usually, however, they talk me into letting them talk about their fathers. I never met a man who couldn't make me fall in love with him by talking about his dad. Even men I truly hate make me love them when that's what they talk about.

MEPHISTOPHELES: Really? Because it turns out my father is the only thing I know how to talk about.

JULIANNA: Okay. You talked me into it. Let's hear it.

MEPHISTOPHELES: Well, to start off, he's a big man. I wish I could show you His suits. What an elegant man He was. Had everything custom made. The linings were always silver and gold. Of course you never saw them because He always kept His jacket buttoned, but you knew the streaks of silver, and the specks of gold were there.

When I was little I was His favorite. He was very busy but He always found time to take me on His knee. Sometimes I would sit and talk to Him while He was getting dressed to go to work. After He'd leave I'd slip my little feet into His wing tips. I don't mind telling you they were far too big for me to fill.

One day He caught me. I had never seen Him so angry. He wasn't the kind of Father to be angry like that but He was.

He threw me out. Said it was time I did more than just play at being Him.

He sent me here. It's been a long time since I've seen Him. He gave me an assignment, to fix things up in a certain territory He'd lost touch with, and not to come back till I did.

I've been trying ever since, using everything He ever taught me but it's hard work. It's a people oriented kind of job. You spend all your time giving people what they want, only to find out they don't know what they want themselves. I miss Him. I wish I could do what He'd do in my place, but you can't always know.

JULIANNA: Is that really what happened?

MEPHISTOPHELES: Every word is true.

JULIANNA: It's lovely.

MEPHISTOPHELES: It's very sad, too, don't you think?

JULIANNA: The stories are always sad when they're about their fathers.

MEPHISTOPHELES: Always?

JULIANNA: Always.

MEPHISTOPHELES: I never thought about it but you're right. You go around thinking you're a special case when you're really just like everybody else.

JULIANNA: I guess you are.

(JULIANNA *kisses* MEPHISTOPHELES. *He pushes her away, genuinely curious.*)

MEPHISTOPHELES: And that's what makes you love men when they talk about their fathers—that they all think they're different but they're really all the same?

JULIANNA: *(She continues kissing him.)* Oh, well, in your case there are some other things I'm...fond of, besides.

MEPHISTOPHELES: *(Pushing her away again)* Would you care to mention them?

JULIANNA: For a guy who can do what you can do you're kind of insecure.

MEPHISTOPHELES: I've got a lot on my mind.

JULIANNA: *(Helping him out of his cape.)*

Maybe I can make you forget.

MEPHISTOPHELES: You'd be the first one who could. *(They lie down together. He turns off the lights with a wave of his hand.)*

JULIANNA: I'll pretend I didn't see that.

(Blackout)

Scene Eight

(Soft lights up on the bed)

(JULIANNA is sitting on the edge of the bed, facing out, wrapped in one of the sheets. MEPHISTOPHELES kneels on the bed directly behind her, wearing nothing we can see.)

JULIANNA: My mother always told me sex was beautiful, in marriage, but I never listened to half of what my mother told me so I didn't really hear the second part.

So you can see why it has never seemed strange to me that no matter who I've ended up lying down with, I always say my prayers before I fall asleep. "Dear God, before I go to sleep" is how I always start my prayer, and then I thank you for a lot of stuff and promise to be better. As you may remember, I never ask you for anything in particular in the body of the prayer, but add it in sort of a postscript. I was taught that to ask you for something directly was impolite. So if I wanted something really important I always sent it up by itself. I always figured this gave you the chance to stop listening if you wanted to.

Saying my prayers used to be hard. My mother used to help me. After awhile when it got easy I figured it should be hard, so I made up some rules so it would be.

I had to say it all in one breath. I had to do it right with no mistakes, and if I made one I had to start all over from the start without taking another breath of air. I had to keep my eyes closed tight no matter how many horrible things would creep up on me out of the dark places that filled my room after my mother turned off the light.

All these things were proof to me that you would hear me. But as I got older I gradually stopped doing them all. When I say my prayers now I breathe as much as I like. If my mind wanders and I lose my place I just back up a few words and start again. I open my eyes, or keep them closed, it no longer matters. The dark worlds that lived in corners and under my bed are gone from me, forever.

Well, that's all right and I don't mind—well, I mind but
it's all right. You don't hear my prayers but I give them
to you anyway. I guess I figure we've kind of got a
deal. I get to say them, if you don't have to hear them.
But I'd like to ask you to hear me now. After all these
years of hearing, or not hearing, the same old prayer,
I've got a new one.
So here it is.

Dear God,
Before I go to sleep I want to thank you for this day
and all its blessings.
Something has happened to me that I think you
must have had a hand in. It feels more like you than
anything I've ever felt. I think all these years you really
must have been listening, because under all my prayers
was the prayer that this thing would happen.
So this is sort of a thank you, but it's more than that.
It's sort of to tell you that while I've never really
believed that it *would* happen, I always believed that it
could. That is, I like believing that I believed. Only now,
it's real.
I don't know if I can do what I'm supposed to do, now
that it's real. But I'll try.
I'm scared. So scared.
That's all.
Amen.

(MEPHISTOPHELES *and* JULIANNA *are surrounded in a
warm, glowing light.*)

MEPHISTOPHELES: Amen.

(Fade to blackout)

Scene Nine

(Early morning. Both JULIANNA *and* MEPHISTOPHELES *are dressed. She paces nervously.)*

JULIANNA: Look, it's just too insane. You think I don't know what happens when a person makes a deal with you but I know.

Excuse me for saying this, but it isn't pretty.

MEPHISTOPHELES: You've been reading too many books.

JULIANNA: There's one or two in particular.

MEPHISTOPHELES: Ah. *(An enormous phone book materializes in his hand.)*

The phone book. *(He gestures, perhaps something magical happens concerning the phone book so that Julianna can see a particular page.)*

Count 'em. Eighty-two Fausts. Eighty-two Fausts in the greater metropolitan area and not one of them carrying on the family business. *(He disposes of the phone book magically.)*

I try to stick with tradition, God knows. I went to all the Fausts first. Made them good, solid offers.

JULIANNA: So they turned you down. That's any reason why you should come messing up my life?

MEPHISTOPHELES: Last night you didn't see it that way.

JULIANNA: Last night was last night. I want to know what will happen to me if I say yes.

MEPHISTOPHELES: You will feel what you felt last night...with Paris.

JULIANNA: Perry? What do you know about Perry!

MEPHISTOPHELES: That you love him.

JULIANNA: If I love him, what was I doing rolling in the hay with you last night?

MEPHISTOPHELES: Figurative hay. Figurative roll.

JULIANNA: Easy for you to say.

MEPHISTOPHELES: I wish it were.

JULIANNA: You could say something else, you know.

MEPHISTOPHELES: I wish I could. But Paris is the one you want to say it.

JULIANNA: Yes. But he doesn't really love me, so it doesn't matter what he says or doesn't say.

MEPHISTOPHELES: That's not true.

JULIANNA: He doesn't.

MEPHISTOPHELES: You don't know that for sure.

JULIANNA: You don't get it, do you? You don't have a clue. If you don't know for sure that someone loves you—if when you look at them, you don't know—then it doesn't matter.

MEPHISTOPHELES: What if you could know for sure? Would that moment be worth your soul?

JULIANNA: One moment...

MEPHISTOPHELES: Yes. Is it worth your soul to have a moment when the love you have together is all, and is enough.

JULIANNA: Yes, but only—

MEPHISTOPHELES: What?

JULIANNA: Only if it's worth Perry's soul too.

MEPHISTOPHELES: It is.

JULIANNA: He doesn't think so.

MEPHISTOPHELES: He's already promised it.

JULIANNA: I wish I could believe you.

MEPHISTOPHELES: Would you like me to show you that he has?

JULIANNA: Show me? How?

MEPHISTOPHELES: Like this. *(He makes a magical gesture.)*

(Blackout)

Scene Ten

(Just before daybreak. JULIANNA *bends over* PARIS' *sleeping form.* MEPHISTOPHELES *hovers in the air over the bed.)*

JULIANNA: How sweet you are when sleeping. All that is unknown about you, gone. *(She strokes his face.)* When you sleep I am the one who must work to make you. If I stop for any instant you disappear. When I sleep beside you, we are gone somewhere together, and when we wake, make ourselves together again.
You are someplace now without me, but I am here with you. Take me with you, Paris. Don't forget me, make me in the world of sleep where you are, as I make you here with me. Find me, Paris.

PARIS: *(Waking, whispering)* Julianna?

JULIANNA: Again.

PARIS: Julianna? *(He begins to embrace her, then sees* MEPHISTOPHELES.*)* WHAT'S HE DOING HERE! *(Leaping out of bed.)*

MEPHISTOPHELES: I told you I'd bring you a woman who'd love you—

PARIS: You mean she's the one—how could you DO this to me!

JULIANNA: You know I love you, Perry.

PARIS: I know, but—

JULIANNA: And you love me—

PARIS: I love you more than I've ever loved anybody, but—

JULIANNA: But what?

PARIS: *(To* MEPHISTOPHELES*)* Look—it's not going to work—she doesn't love me enough.

JULIANNA: Don't say that, Perry.

PARIS: You don't, Julie, you just don't—I'm not saying you don't love me a lot, I'm not saying that, but if you loved me enough, Julie—don't you see, if you loved me enough—

JULIANNA: I do.

MEPHISTOPHELES: She does.

PARIS: You don't understand.

MEPHISTOPHELES: The last three nights I've seen how much she loves you.

PARIS: The last three—you've been going to *her* all this time? I left her to be with you and you left me to go to her? I don't believe you did that to me!

MEPHISTOPHELES: I did it for you—and for her, too.

PARIS: Like hell you did. *(To* JULIANNA*)* I didn't know he was going to you!

MEPHISTOPHELES: Who else could I have gotten to love you—your mother?

PARIS: Listen Buster—you leave my mother out of this!

JULIANNA: Perry, look at me and—

PARIS: Julie, it's not going to work. It's just not. You don't—

MEPHISTOPHELES: She loves you. Enough.

PARIS: Oh yeah? Then what was she doing with you last night—and the night before—and the night before that— *(To* JULIANNA*)* If you loved me enough—

JULIANNA: What is enough, Perry? What? Tell me and that's now much I'll love you.

PARIS: I—don't know. I just know that however much—

JULIANNA: Tell me, Perry. Now.

PARIS: I TOLD YOU I DON'T KNOW!

JULIANNA: Then you find out.

PARIS: What if I find out and you can't? What if it's too much for you?

JULIANNA: Try me.

PARIS: But—

JULIANNA: No buts. I'm here saying yes.
I'm saying I'll try to love you, as much, in any way, in every place and every time as you can think of ways for me to love you.

(PARIS *stands still for an instant. Then he embraces* JULIANNA *almost violently, clinging to her.*)

MEPHISTOPHELES: Then it's worth your soul to love him?

JULIANNA: Yes. (*A small, magical sound is heard.*)

MEPHISTOPHELES: And yours, Paris?

PARIS: Yes. (*Again, the small magical sound. A long scrolled contract descends, and a quill pen floats down from above. Mephistopheles floats above Paris and Julianna, who sign the contract.*)

MEPHISTOPHELES: Let it be known that Paris, and Julianna, who stand before God, and this company, have pledged their souls for one moment of perfect love.

(*Sustained horn blast*)

MEPHISTOPHELES: And if these two should join
in perfect desire on the surface of earth, then the
heavens will rejoice. And God's hidden grace
will be uncovered, the forgotten promises will be
remembered, and everywhere we look will show the
glory of His face.
Even I will shield my eyes from that pure light when
the great binding sorrow of the heart's one true desire
will be broken. Because we will all be like Him. At last,
we will all be like Him. And I will go and stand before
Him, with your radiance on my hands.
To Paris and Julianna, who stand before God, and this
company and who pledge their souls to tempt eternal
grace I say—

(Sustained horn blast)

MEPHISTOPHELES: Amen.

(Blackout)

END OF ACT ONE

ACT TWO

The Honeymoon

(JULIANNA *and* PARIS's *apartments have joined together, creating one whole apartment. They sit on the king bed that has replaced their twin beds. She is wearing pajama tops, and he is wearing pajama bottoms.*)

(MEPHISTOPHELES *strolls on stage. To the audience*)

MEPHISTOPHELES: The Honeymoon. (*He reaches the bed.*) On the first night... (*He drops on all fours and jumps up on the foot of the bed. He snaps his fingers.*)

(*The sound of a great waterfall, thundering close by, an occasional mist spraying.*)

(JULIANNA *or* PARIS *or both are suddenly wearing yellow foul weather gear type hats that say* MAID OF THE MIST—NIAGARA FALLS.)

PARIS: Uhhh—

JULIANNA: Uhhh—we were thinking, uhhh, more tropical—

(MEPHISTOPHELES *snaps his fingers.*)

(*The sound of the surf, seagulls, ukulele, someone singing Aloha, etc.*)

(JULIANNA *or* PARIS *or both may be wearing leis.*)

(*Paris whispers to her, she nods, agreeing*)

JULIANNA: Maybe a bit...more...romantic?

(MEPHISTOPHELES *snaps his fingers. The lights dim.*)

PARIS: *(Man to man type talk)* What Julie meant was, we'd like to be alone now, okay?

(MEPHISTOPHELES *snaps his fingers. The music and singing stops, leaving only the sound of the surf and gulls. The lights dim further.*)

PARIS: No, uhhh, she meant alone...get it? We'd like to be—

(MEPHISTOPHELES *snaps his fingers again. The surf and gulls stop. The lights dim further.*)

PARIS: ALONE!! We want to be—

(MEPHISTOPHELES *snaps his fingers. The lights black.*)

(A beat. In the darkness, PARIS sighs.)

PARIS: At last.

(There is a thumping sound, like a dog scratching)

PARIS: What's that?

JULIANNA: What?

(The thumping continues.)

PARIS: That sound.

JULIANNA: That?

PARIS: Yes, that.

JULIANNA: Sounds like a dog.

Sounds like a poodle...

PARIS: A poodle...

(JULIANNA *and* PARIS *listen for several seconds.*)

(PARIS *switches on the light.*)

(MEPHISTOPHELES *is scratching himself with one of his legs like a dog. He is wearing some poodle characteristics.*)

PARIS: That's supposed to be a poodle? Looks more like a great dane with a permanent to me. *(He reaches for the poodles red collar, and reads the tag.)* "My name is Sam." His name is Sam now. "If lost, please return to Dad." Very funny.

(MEPHISTOPHELES continues to scratch and thump.)

PARIS: Well, we'll just pretend he isn't here. This is our honeymoon, we'll just go ahead, go right ahead and do what we—what we— *(He starts to move toward Julianna's side of the bed, to embrace her, then doesn't.)*

JULIANNA: Well.

PARIS: Well.

(JULIANNA and PARIS stare front for several seconds.)

JULIANNA: Here we are.

PARIS: Yes. Here we are.

(JULIANNA and PARIS freeze.)

(MEPHISTOPHELES lifts his head.)

MEPHISTOPHELES: On the second night. *(He lies back down. He has become slightly more of a poodle. He curls up on his side.)*

(JULIANNA and PARIS are sitting, facing front.)

PARIS: *(Hesitantly)* Sam? *(He prods MEPHISTOPHELES with his foot.)* Sam?
I think he's asleep.

JULIANNA: All he's done so far is sleep.

PARIS: I wanted to ask him something.

JULIANNA: What?

PARIS: How we're supposed to do it.

JULIANNA: Oh?

JULIANNA & PARIS: Sam? *(Near panic)* SAM!!!! *(No response. They sink back against the headboard.)*

JULIANNA: *(Forced cheerfulness)* Well...sweet dreams.

PARIS: *(Strained, but also forced brightness)* Pleasant sleep.

(JULIANNA and PARIS freeze.)

(MEPHISTOPHELES lifts his head.)

MEPHISTOPHELES: On the third night. (He lies back down, even more of a poodle.

(JULIANNA lays her head down, and is sleeping.)

(PARIS crawls to the foot of the bed and starts shaking MEPHISTOPHELES. Whispering loudly)

PARIS: Sam! Sam, please, I—

(JULIANNA wakes, sees what PARIS is doing. He sees that she sees.)

PARIS: Oh.

JULIANNA: *(Whispering)* I was up all last night trying that.

PARIS: *(Whispering)* You think there's something wrong with him?

JULIANNA: *(Whispering)* I don't know.

PARIS: *(Crawling back up to the head of the bed, getting under the covers. Still whispering)* What do you think we should do?

JULIANNA: *(Whispering)* I don't know

(JULIANNA and PARIS both sink back under the covers, and end up face to face. They kiss, instinctively. As they begin to embrace, they pull apart, looking in the direction of the foot of the bed. They sink down under the covers, as far apart as possible, staring front.)

(They freeze.)

MEPHISTOPHELES: *(Raises his head)* On the fourth night. *(And lies back down, having added more poodle attributes.)*

(JULIANNA and PARIS move slowly towards each other and kiss, embracing.)

(They look at each other, then at MEPHISTOPHELES, shrug, and kiss again.)

(They both check MEPHISTOPHELES to see if he's watching. He seems to be just curled up, a regular dog)

(Kiss, and check again.)

(Kiss for a long time, then pull the covers over themselves, and continue their lovemaking, hidden.)

(MEPHISTOPHELES lifts his head, turns to look at them. Smiles)

MEPHISTOPHELES: On the fifth night. *(He lies back down, even more of a poodle.)*

(Voluptuous noises float out from under the covers.)

(JULIANNA and PARIS come out from under the covers eating a large take out pizza.)

JULIANNA: What do you think it will be like?

PARIS: You want the last piece?

JULIANNA: No, it's yours.

PARIS: We'll split it.
I don't know.

JULIANNA: I think about it all the time.

PARIS: Yeah, me too.

JULIANNA: Yeah.

(JULIANNA and PARIS eat for several moments)

JULIANNA: When do you think it will happen?

PARIS: Soon.

JULIANNA: You really think so?

PARIS: Yeah. I do.

(PARIS *pulls* JULIANNA *to him, they embrace.*)

(*They freeze.*)

MEPHISTOPHELES: (*Raises his head*) On the sixth night. (*He lies back down, almost completely a poodle.*)

PARIS: (*Sits up, breaking the embrace*) Why doesn't it happen?

JULIANNA: Come on, sweetheart, go back to sleep.

PARIS: No. I want to know why it doesn't happen. I want him to tell me. Hey. Sam!

(PARIS *kicks* MEPHISTOPHELES, *who makes no response.*)

PARIS: Sam! I want you to tell me why it doesn't happen! (*Kicks him again and again*) SAM!!!

JULIANNA: Perry stop—don't hurt him—

PARIS: I want to know why.

JULIANNA: Maybe we're not trying hard enough— maybe we—

PARIS: But we have, Julie, we have.
What are we going to do?

JULIANNA: We could—we could have a child.

PARIS: You think—you think that if we wanted a child it might—

JULIANNA: Oh, Perry, don't think like that. Just think about having a child.

PARIS: I think I'd like to. Wouldn't you?

JULIANNA: I would.

PARIS: So would I.

JULIANNA: You do?

PARIS: Yes.

(JULIANNA *and* PARIS *start to embrace.*)

PARIS: But—

JULIANNA: But what, Perry? It's easy.

PARIS: No it's not.

JULIANNA: Yes, it is. Millions of people do it every day.

PARIS: But what about—what about Sam—

JULIANNA: He never said we couldn't.

PARIS: I know, but—

JULIANNA: So we can.
We can do whatever we want.
Don't worry about Sam, Perry.

PARIS: But—

JULIANNA: You know what I think sometimes? I think he's just a dog.

(JULIANNA *and* PARIS *embrace.*)

(Freeze)

MEPHISTOPHELES: *(Raising his head)* And on the seventh night—

(JULIANNA *and* PARIS *lie in each other's arms.*)

(MEPHISTOPHELES *puts on the final piece of his poodle disguise, and howls.*)

(As the lights black, spot on MEPHISTOPHELES.*)*

MEPHISTOPHELES: The honeymoon's over.

(Blackout)

Scene One

(JULIANNA *and* PARIS *are in bed.*)

(JULIANNA *picks up Proust's* Remembrance of Things Past. *She reads it throughout the second act, and except when she is sleeping, the large black hardbound book lies open in her lap.*)

(PARIS *picks up nail clippers and a newspaper, which he spreads out near the foot of his side of the bed. He clips his nails throughout the second act, unless sleeping, or talking to* MEPHISTOPHELES.)

(MEPHISTOPHELES, *as Sam, lies curled up at the foot of the bed.*)

(*Downstage from the bed is a smaller bed, surrounded by toys, children's books, scattered clothing.* MARGARET *is asleep there, under the covers.*)

(*Paris is watching T V. The bluish white light, dancing from the images on the screen, is reflected on his and* JULIANNA's *faces.*)

PARIS: What's happening now, anyway?

JULIANNA: Here? He's waiting for his mother to kiss him goodnight.

PARIS: Sounds boring.

JULIANNA: No, actually, it's one of the most famous parts of the book.

PARIS: I thought the thing with the cookie, the little French cookie, what's it called—he takes a bite and his past comes blasting back, I thought that was the most famous.

JULIANNA: Yes, but this is too.

PARIS: How long has he been waiting?

JULIANNA: 5 pages.

PARIS: Wow. I'll stick with T V. *(He continues to focus on the T V. After a few moments)* Oh— *(He points.)* You got to be putting me on! Did you see that?!?

JULIANNA: What?

PARIS: What the guy in the hat did.

JULIANNA: No, what?

PARIS: He did it again!

JULIANNA: What!?!

PARIS: Aw, shit, a commercial.

*(*MARGARET *whines and whimpers.* MEPHISTOPHELES *looks in her direction, crawls a few inches closer.)*

PARIS: Do you think Sam's been scratching a lot lately?

JULIANNA: Seems all right to me. It doesn't to you?

PARIS: He does it a lot, in the middle of the night. Keeps me up.

JULIANNA: Doesn't me.

PARIS: Last night I didn't get any sleep at all.

JULIANNA: You were sound asleep when I turned out the light.

PARIS: Yeah, well, I woke up right after. He waits till you're asleep before he starts. It's not the scratching that bothers me so much. It's the thumping. Thump thump thump. I can't get any sleep. What kind of life is this when you can't get any sleep?

JULIANNA: It never used to bother you.

PARIS: Sam didn't used to do it.

JULIANNA: He did too.

PARIS: Thump thump thump

(Sam scratches, thump, thump, thump.)

JULIANNA: You're turning into the Prince and the Pea.

PARIS: I think we should make him sleep in the kitchen.

JULIANNA: It's too late to make him sleep in the kitchen. He's always slept in here.
Oh—it's started again.

(JULIANNA *and* PARIS *watch for several moments*)

PARIS: You know, that actor has always reminded me of him.

JULIANNA: Who?

PARIS: You know who I mean.

JULIANNA: The mailman reminds you of him.

PARIS: Don't you think he looks a little like him?

(MARGARET *can be heard crying.* MEPHISTOPHELES *whimpers, and scratches the bed.*)

JULIANNA: No. Not at all. He was Italian looking.

PARIS: Italian? Italian? He was this big. He had blue eyes.

JULIANNA: Forget it, Perry.

PARIS: What are you talking about, Italian looking?

JULIANNA: Look, I don't remember what he looked like, okay?

PARIS: Then why did you say he was Italian looking? You really think he did?

JULIANNA: Perry, please. I said I don't remember.

(MARGARET's *crying gets louder.* MEPHISTOPHELES *jumps off the bed, takes a step towards her room, then stops, jumps back on the bed.*)

(JULIANNA *and* PARIS *watch T V for several moments.*)

PARIS: I think I hear her.

JULIANNA: (*Tilts her head to one side, listens, nods her head*) Yeah, I'll go. (*She starts to throw back the covers.*)

PARIS: No, she's stopped.

(JULIANNA *settles back into bed.* JULIANNA *and* PARIS *watch T V for several moments.*)

(*They sigh.* PARIS *clicks off the T V with the remote control switch.*)

JULIANNA: Sweet dreams.

PARIS: Pleasant sleep.

(JULIANNA *and* PARIS *kiss and lie down to sleep.*)

(PARIS *waits until he thinks that* JULIANNA *is asleep, then crawls to the foot of the bed, grabs Sam, pulls him off the bed and downstage.*)

(*He speaks in a loud stage whisper at first.*)

PARIS: Sam. Sam. I've got to talk to you about something important. Sam—

(*Sam does some dog business, completely ignoring* PARIS.)

PARIS: Sam, I am getting tired of this. I'm getting tired of talking to you all the time and never getting an answer.

You see, Sam, my mother is real sick, and—

(PARIS *waits for some response from Sam, there is none.*)

PARIS: Okay. Okay, if that's the way you want it, okay. I guess I don't have any business talking to you about this in the first place. I should be talking to Him— (*He gestures, above.*) —but I figured, as long as you're right here, why rack up those long distance charges.
That was a joke.

You're a tough audience, you know that, Sam? One tough audience. Or maybe it's my material. Is it my material, Sam? Go on, you can tell me. I can take it.

(*Sam lies down on his side.* PARIS *sits down next to him.*)

PARIS: You know, death is kind of like a joke. Yeah.
Like a dirty joke some older kid tells you when you're
too young to get it, but you laugh all the same. You
laugh and laugh and you have absolutely no idea why
it's supposed to be funny but you know that someday,
when you grow up, you'll get it.
But I don't get it. My mother is dying, Sam, and I don't
get it. I know I'm supposed to. I already know all the
punch lines—here—let me try a few of them out on
you:
She had a good life.
Be thankful for the time you had together.
Think of all the joy you must have given her, don't use
her death to rob her of the joy she's given you.
I could go on, but you get the general idea.
See, what I think—what I really think is, that if you
love someone enough then they shouldn't have to die.
I don't know if that means they die because we don't
love them enough or not.
But the joke would certainly be on us if that's why,
wouldn't it? If they die just because we don't love them
enough.
Yes. It would be quite a joke.

(PARIS *goes back to bed. Sam follows.*)

(*There is the sound of* MARGARET *crying softly as* PARIS
kisses JULIANNA.)

PARIS: Pleasant sleep. (*He lies down to sleep.*)

(MARGARET *sits huddles in the middle of her little bed with
the covers all wrapped around her, whimpering and shaking.
She decides to make a run for it. She throws off the covers
and dashes to her parents' bed. She gets to her mother's side
and stops abruptly. She bends over* JULIANNA. *She reaches
out her hand, but does not touch* JULIANNA.)

MARGARET: *(Whispering)* Mommy? Mommy? You asleep? *(Louder)* Mommy? Mommy?

(JULIANNA stirs. MARGARET bends closer.)

MARGARET: Mommy?

JULIANNA: *(Wakes, pulls away from MARGARET, frightened, stifling a scream)* NO!!! Leave us alone, leave us— *(She sees that it is MARGARET, and calms down.)* Oh...it's you.

MARGARET: What's wrong, Mommy, it's me.

JULIANNA: It's all right, baby, I thought you were someone else.

MARGARET: But it's just me. Are you all right?

JULIANNA: Yes, I'm okay.

MARGARET: You frightened me.

JULIANNA: *You* frightened *me.*

(JULIANNA holds out her arms. MARGARET comes to her.)

JULIANNA: What's the matter?

MARGARET: I got scared.

JULIANNA: Of what?

MARGARET: I had a bad dream again.

JULIANNA: A bad dream? Was it so awful?

MARGARET: Yes. They were trying to hurt me.

JULIANNA: Who?

MARGARET: They were.

JULIANNA: Darling, your dreams can't hurt you.

MARGARET: Yes they can.

JULIANNA: I'm here. You don't have to be afraid.

MARGARET: You're here but you're not in my room.

JULIANNA: It's two little steps away.

MARGARET: It's too far away.

JULIANNA: You're a big girl now. Too big to sleep with your mother and father.

MARGARET: Then can you come in with me? Daddy won't mind, he doesn't get scared.

JULIANNA: We've talked about the dark, remember? What did we say about the dark?

MARGARET: That if we say our prayers it will go away?

JULIANNA: No, darling, it doesn't go away. It—

MARGARET: I *know* it doesn't go away.

JULIANNA: Shall I say your prayers with you? Will that make it better? Will that help?

JULIANNA & MARGARET:
Dear God.
Before I go to sleep I want to thank you for this day and all its blessings, for Mommy and Daddy are dear ones.
If I've done anything wrong, I'm sorry. Please forgive me.
Send me sweet dreams and pleasant sleep, so that tomorrow I may wake up, eager and strong, to do what is good, and hate what is bad.
Amen.

JULIANNA: *(Kissing her)* Better now?

MARGARET: A little.

JULIANNA: Go on, then. Remember you're a big girl. I'm right here. Go on. *(Kisses her again)* Sweet dreams.

MARGARET: Pleasant sleep.

(MARGARET *leaves,* JULIANNA *watches her go.*)

(*As* MARGARET *approaches her room she hesitates, then breaks into a full run and jumps onto her bed. She bundles up in the covers again, and sits, shaking.*)

(JULIANNA *sighs, and lies back down.*)

(*A few moments later* MARGARET *is crying softly again.*)

(MEPHISTOPHELES *jumps off the bed, he's anxious to go to her, but he doesn't, he returns to his post.*)

(PARIS *starts to toss and turn,* JULIANNA *reaches out and puts her hand on his shoulder.*)

JULIANNA: Can't you sleep?

PARIS: No.

JULIANNA: Me neither.
Thinking about your mother.

PARIS: Yes.

JULIANNA: Me too.
There's nothing you can do about it, Perry.

PARIS: I know.

JULIANNA: Nothing.

PARIS: Okay.

JULIANNA: Nothing he can do either.

PARIS: Come on, Julie—

JULIANNA: He can't.

PARIS: Okay. OKAY.

JULIANNA: Not okay.

PARIS: Will you just stop? Just stop, okay?

JULIANNA: Sam, come here—

PARIS: Leave him alone—

JULIANNA: Sam...come on, boy, come on—

(*Sam crawls up to the head of the bed.*)

JULIANNA: That's a good boy—now, Sam—roll over.

(*Sam rolls over.*)

PARIS: What do you think you're doing?

JULIANNA: Good Boy. Now, Sam, sit.

(Sam sits.)

JULIANNA: Sam, beg.

(Sam begs.)

JULIANNA: Sam, shake.

(Sam shakes.)

JULIANNA: Sam...make Perry's mother young again.

(Sam sits there quietly, head tilted to one side.)

PARIS: *(Gets out of bed, angry)* Why won't you stop!

JULIANNA: I'm here, Perry. I'm here, and there's no one else.

PARIS: I need him—

JULIANNA: He can't help us, Perry! We're on our own. Nothing that he can do or say makes any difference. It's just you and me, sweetheart. You and me and Margaret. The three of us. That's all there is.

PARIS: You don't understand!

JULIANNA: Then you'll make me. *(She sighs.)*
Sweet dreams.

(PARIS does not respond.)

JULIANNA: Sweet dreams, Perry.
All right then. Goodnight. *(She turns away from him and settles down to sleep.)*

(PARIS paces for several moments. He stops, several feet from the bed, and talks to himself, in a cross between laughter and tears.)

PARIS: She had a good life.
Be thankful for the time you had together.

Think of all the joy you must have given her. Don't use...her death... *(He does not continue.)*

(PARIS sighs, wipes away the tears, and goes back to bed. He starts clipping his toenails.)

(JULIANNA is reading.)

JULIANNA: You didn't like the way I cooked the chicken, did you?

PARIS: Julia, anyone can cook a chicken.

JULIANNA: Not like your mother can, they can't. *(Pause)* I mean, well, you know what I mean. I mean your mother's chicken is—I mean was...

PARIS: It's okay.

JULIANNA: No, it is not okay. I made the chicken so it would taste like your mother's chicken.
Now the fact of the matter is that I really, truly liked the way your mother's chicken tasted, but that is not the point.
I should have made meatloaf.

PARIS: You make terrible meatloaf. Your meatloaf is almost as bad as your chicken.

JULIANNA: Yeah, but at least it wouldn't have reminded you of your mother.
Things remind you of your mother too much.
I wonder if I can get Sam to eat it. I can't just throw it away.

PARIS: I wouldn't count on it. He got sick the last time you tried to give him some of your chicken.

JULIANNA: I got a special roasting chicken. It isn't cheap, you know.

PARIS: Let's not worry about it just now.

JULIANNA: Perry, we have to worry about it sooner or later.

PARIS: Then later.

JULIANNA: Now.

PARIS: Not now.

JULIANNA: Now.

PARIS: *(Throws the covers off, swings his feet off the bed.)* I'd better let the dog out.

JULIANNA: You let him out ten times already. *(Holding him back)*

PARIS: I have to be alone on this one, okay?

JULIANNA: You're alone too much.

PARIS: You don't understand.

JULIANNA: I understand I just burned a chicken into oblivion that we can't afford to burn because you didn't call me when the buzzer went off. I asked you ten times if I asked you once to call me when the buzzer went off. You were right there.

PARIS: I didn't think. I heard it but I forgot. All it cost us is the chicken, okay?

JULIANNA: Not okay.

PARIS: Look—everything reminds me of her. When we're together I just think about her more. Sometimes I just like to make it all go away.

JULIANNA: All the time, Perry, is when you like it.

PARIS: It's not right. I know it's not. I should be able to just go on, like other people do. I don't know anyone anymore this hasn't happened to and they go on. Some of them are alone. I have you. They'll all alone. And they go on.

JULIANNA: And so will you.

PARIS: If things had been different—

JULIANNA: Things aren't different. Your mother loved you. You loved your mother. That's not something you would have wanted different.

(MARGARET *is crying, softly, in her room.*)

(MEPHISTOPHELES *looks in her direction, but does not go to her.*)

PARIS: That's not what I meant. I meant if things had been different with us—if we had been able to have—

JULIANNA: Stop it, Perry.

PARIS: You're not even trying anymore, are you?

JULIANNA: Everything I do every day I do because I love you and Margaret as much as I can.

PARIS: How could I forget! A saint and martyr, that's what you are.

JULIANNA: Well, compared to you I am!

PARIS: Don't pretend you don't know what I'm talking about it. If we could, somehow, have had what he promised us—

JULIANNA: It wasn't real, Perry. It was just something we both remember.

PARIS: It happened.

JULIANNA: Fine. It happened. We had a crazy dream together. It doesn't change things about your mother—or pay the bills.

PARIS: Why do you say things like that!

JULIANNA: Because you're driving me crazy! Who cares what he promised us. What we have is enough.

PARIS: No, it's not enough—

JULIANNA: It is for me!

PARIS: I'm trying so hard—doesn't that matter to you?

JULIANNA: Of course, but—

PARIS: Don't you think that if I could—if *we* could—
don't you think I know it's not your fault, it's mine?
Don't you think I know that, Julianna!

(JULIANNA *looks away.*)

(PARIS *gradually sinks back down, into quietness.*)

(MARGARET *is still crying.*)

(They both lie there, listening.)

PARIS: She's crying again.
Why is she so frightened of the dark?

JULIANNA: Because everybody is.

(JULIANNA *and* PARIS *listen.*)

(MARGARET *stops crying.*)

PARIS: Goodnight.

JULIANNA: Goodnight.

(JULIANNA *and* PARIS *lie down, facing away from each
other, and go to sleep.*)

(MARGARET *starts crying again.*)

(MEPHISTOPHELES *jumps up off the bed, then anxiously
circles it. Hesitates, then goes into* MARGARET's *room. He
jumps on* MARGARET's *bed, and that instant transforms
back into* MEPHISTOPHELES.)

MEPHISTOPHELES: Don't be frightened. It's just me, Sam.

MARGARET: Sam.

MEPHISTOPHELES: You shouldn't have given me your
vegetables. It keeps me up at night.

MARGARET: But you always eat them.

MEPHISTOPHELES: They're not good for dogs, they're
good for you.

MARGARET: I always knew you could talk. I tell mom
that all the time.

MEPHISTOPHELES: And what does she say?

MARGARET: She says for me to eat my vegetables.

MEPHISTOPHELES: What's all this crying about, anyway? Did you have a bad dream?

MARGARET: It was horrible.

MEPHISTOPHELES: Tell me about it. Sometimes that makes it go away.

MARGARET: It will just come back.

MEPHISTOPHELES: If it does, you know what you should say to it?

MARGARET: What?

MEPHISTOPHELES: You just say, "Sam said for you to go away."

MARGARET: And will bad dreams go because you say so?

MEPHISTOPHELES: Of course. They know me very well.

MARGARET: Will you stay with me tonight so they won't come back?

MEPHISTOPHELES: I can't.

MARGARET: Why not?

MEPHISTOPHELES: Sleeping at the foot of your parents' bed is my job. You wouldn't want me not to do my job, would you?

MARGARET: I just don't want to have another bad dream. My mother said they can't hurt me but I know that's not true.

MEPHISTOPHELES: Your mother doesn't know everything.

MARGARET: Oh yes she does. She just says that so I won't be afraid. She knows it isn't really true.
Can't you stay just this once? I won't tell. I promise.

MEPHISTOPHELES: No.

MARGARET: But I'm so scared at night sometimes.

MEPHISTOPHELES: I could sing to you. Would you like that? I'm very famous for my songs.

MARGARET: You mean, instead of staying?

MEPHISTOPHELES: I cannot stay.

MARGARET: My mother used to sing to me, when I was little.

MEPHISTOPHELES: When you were little?

MARGARET: I'm a big girl now.

MEPHISTOPHELES: I don't know if a big girl like you would like my singing.

MARGARET: *(Laughing)* You're just teasing me. I can tell. You're going to sing.

MEPHISTOPHELES: All right. Just this once. You promise not to tell your parents?

MARGARET: Cross my heart and hope to die. Stick a needle in my—

MEPHISTOPHELES: I believe you. I believe you.
(He cradles MARGARET *in his arms, and sings softly.)*
Hush little baby, don't say a word
Pappa's gonna buy you a mockingbird.
If that mockingbird don't sing
Pappa's gonna buy you a diamond ring.
If that diamond ring turns to brass
Pappa's gonna buy you a looking glass.
If that looking glass gets broke
Pappa's gonna buy you a billy goat.

*(*MEPHISTOPHELES *begins to hum, as* MARGARET *gets very, very sleepy.)*

MARGARET: I can't wait for daddy to buy me a billy goat.

MEPHISTOPHELES: It's just a song, Margaret.

MARGARET: You mean he's not going to buy me one?

MEPHISTOPHELES: The fact is that goats are awfully hard to keep in an apartment.

MARGARET: It's so mean! Why does everybody sing you songs where they promise you things they're not going to give you?

(MEPHISTOPHELES *holds* MARGARET *close.*)

MEPHISTOPHELES: I don't know.

PARIS: *(Sits up in bed, whispers)* Sam...Sam... *(Doesn't see him at the foot of the bed, looks for him)* Come on, Sam, I know you're here somewhere. *(Gets up, looks under bed, etc.)*

(MEPHISTOPHELES *continues to hum, watching* MARGARET *while she sleeps.)*

PARIS: Sam, I've got to talk to you—

JULIANNA: *(Awake, watching him)* You know what, Perry?

PARIS: Oh. I was just—

JULIANNA: I know what you were doing, Perry.

PARIS: I couldn't sleep—Sam was scratching and—

JULIANNA: I said I know.

PARIS: You never said anything.

JULIANNA: What would you have liked me to say?

PARIS: Something. Anything.
But I guess you've had your hands full pretending to be asleep.

JULIANNA: I'm not the one pretending, Perry.

PARIS: Oh, right. My department. Self-delusion is my department. Right.

JULIANNA: I meant I haven't been pretending to be asleep while you talk to him.
I've been pretending that you're talking to me.
But that's not all I pretend.
When you're through telling Sam all the things I wish you were telling me, I lie in this bed beside you and pretend that I'm talking to you about all the things I pretended you were talking to me about.
That's a lot of pretending, isn't it?

PARIS: Why didn't you say something, Julie? Why didn't you just—

JULIANNA: I guess I thought I'd get it right. I guess I thought that sooner or later I'd pretend all those things so well that I wouldn't need to say anything out loud to you.
I wouldn't need to say anything at all.
But it's getting worse, lately, not better. Now, whenever I pretend that we're talking together, the way I have to pretend that we do, I always start to cry.

PARIS: Don't cry, Julie, don't.

JULIANNA: You'll have to do better than that. Nobody ever wants you to cry, but they generally do a better job persuading you than Julie, don't cry.
My mother didn't want me crying either, of course, and what she did was come into my room, take me in her arms, and say "What are you crying for, Julie, there are much bigger things to cry about. Much bigger things down the line that will make you want to cry, don't use it all up." And she made me name all the things that didn't make me cry, and while she listened, I stopped crying. But as soon as she left me alone I named all the big things that would make me cry, down the line, and I cried for them. I cried for all the big things that would make me cry.

Don't make me cry over this, Perry. It's not on the list.
Don't make me cry over this.

PARIS: I wonder how many times in a person's life they
say they're sorry?
I wonder if they've done studies.

JULIANNA: Don't, Perry. Don't make me laugh.

PARIS: Would you rather cry?
You have to admit it is funny, you know. A man
talking to his dog while his wife pretends he's talking
to her? I mean, it is funny, isn't it?

JULIANNA: Not if it's happening to you.

PARIS: Oh. Well, how about this—would it be funny if
a person had a husband who used to talk to their dog,
while she pretended he was talking to her? What if it
wasn't happening but used to?

JULIANNA: Still not funny.

PARIS: Okay, how about this. This person *used* to have
a husband who pretended to talk to his wife by talking
to his dog, while she pretended he was talking to her.
How's that? Funny?

JULIANNA: No. It's sad.

PARIS: It is, isn't it. *(Softly)* I'm sorry.

JULIANNA: Yes, but what does it change? You're sorry.
You're sorry about this, you're sorry about that. You're
sorry for everything but the one thing you should be
sorry about.
You don't think I love you enough.
So nothing changes.
You said "You don't love me enough" and you're not
sorry.

PARIS: That was a long time ago—

JULIANNA: Maybe. But you still want me to love you
more. You want me to love you in some other way—a
way that isn't different from the way I love you, but is
somehow better.

PARIS: And you don't? You don't want the same thing
from me? Answer me, Julie—don't you want it too?
And isn't that what we're here doing, wanting more?

JULIANNA: Yes, but—

PARIS: All right then—

JULIANNA: And no—

PARIS: You can't have it both ways.
We both want it. We both want what he promised us.

JULIANNA: He never promised. He only said that if we
tried—

PARIS: We both still want it.

JULIANNA: And nothing changes. I wish it had never
happened.

PARIS: Don't say that—

JULIANNA: Why not? We'd be happy if he hadn't come
along and—

PARIS: You don't know that for sure.

JULIANNA: I do.

PARIS: No you don't. Without him, we might be
married to completely different people. And we
wouldn't have had Margaret, and—

JULIANNA: You're saying we wouldn't have gotten
married? Is that what you're saying?

PARIS: I—I don't know, Julie. Who knows what would
have happened? We can't go back in time and erase
the things he promised us, right? The things he made
us want? The things he whispered to us, in the night.
If he hadn't come along and whispered those things,

I—I might have married Elaine, remember, I told
you stories about Elaire, silly, sweet, my high school
sweetheart. You might have married that guy—what
was his name, thick necked, no sense of humor, what
was his name, the stockbroker—

JULIANNA: Frank, you know his name is Frank.

PARIS: Yeah, you might have married Frank. That's all
I'm saying. If he hadn't whispered things to us—but
he did. So we'll never know. *(Pause)* Tell you what. I'll
stop if you'll stop first.

JULIANNA: No. I don't want to.

PARIS: You're sure?

JULIANNA: Yes. I don't want to ever stop trying. Even if
it makes us miserable, sometimes. And I'm not sorry.

PARIS: Isn't that funny? Neither am I.

(JULIANNA and PARIS kiss.)

(Perhaps there is a sound. Magical, and brief)

*(MEPHISTOPHELES looks in their direction, as if he's heard
something, from very far away.)*

JULIANNA: *(Laughing softly, as they embrace)* You know
what?

PARIS: What?

JULIANNA: Now I think it's funny.

PARIS: What—oh, that. Yeah, I guess it was.

(JULIANNA and PARIS continue to make love.)

*(MEPHISTOPHELES rushes into their bedroom, hurriedly
putting on his Sam costume. He stares at them from beside
the bed.)*

(MARGARET cries softly.)

*(MEPHISTOPHELES takes off whatever portions of his poodle
costume he had managed to slip on, and with the rest of the*

costume, assembles "Sam" at the foot of JULIANNA *and* PARIS's *bed.)*

*(*MEPHISTOPHELES *goes into* MARGARET's *room, and sits on or floats above the headboard of her bed. She is under the sheets, sobbing. He throws off the bedclothes, magically.)*

MEPHISTOPHELES: Caught you again.

MARGARET: *(10 years old)* I was trying to be soooo quiet. They didn't hear me, did they?

MEPHISTOPHELES: No.

MARGARET: Too bad.

MEPHISTOPHELES: If you want them to hear you, Margaret, then cry louder.

MARGARET: You wouldn't understand.
Are you going to sing to me tonight?

MEPHISTOPHELES: If you like.

MARGARET: I'd rather hear a story.

MEPHISTOPHELES: What kind of story?

MARGARET: Any kind of story—as long as it isn't a story with a girl in it my age. I hate those kinds of stories.

MEPHISTOPHELES: The kind of stories they tell you at school?

MARGARET: Yes. They read them to you during quiet time. We have to sit there real quiet with our heads on our desks like slugs while they read them to us. The boys and girls in all the stories are always astronauts or time travelers or pioneer children whose parents have died in avalanches. None of the children ever do anything that any of us are ever going to get to do except maybe at Disneyland, so who the hell cares—

MEPHISTOPHELES: Do they tell you stories about that too, Margaret?

MARGARET: About what—

MEPHISTOPHELES: About hell.

JULIANNA: *(She doesn't look up from her book.)* His mother just kissed him.

PARIS: Great.

JULIANNA: No, it's not.

PARIS: Why not?

JULIANNA: He went a whole night waiting for her to come up to his room and kiss him. She didn't come up till the next night.

PARIS: So? So she missed a night.

JULIANNA: So, he didn't die. He didn't die because she didn't come up and kiss him.

PARIS: So?

MEPHISTOPHELES: Hell is a real place, you know.

MARGARET: Oh, I know. It's below.

(MARGARET is now 12 years old.)

MEPHISTOPHELES: Below—you mean, it's under your bed—

(MEPHISTOPHELES looks under her bed. MARGARET begins to giggle.)

MEPHISTOPHELES: Come out, come out, where ever you are—

MARGARET: Stop it, you're so silly—

MEPHISTOPHELES: *(Sits back up)* No hell under there. I looked.

MARGARET: It's not under my bed, silly.

MEPHISTOPHELES: You're sure?

MARGARET: Well, sometimes you sort of think it is, but it isn't, really.

MEPHISTOPHELES: Then where is it?

MARGARET: Below us, you know, below.

MEPHISTOPHELES: You mean, under the house? You mean that if I start to dig— *(A shovel appears in his hands, he starts to dig.)*

MARGARET: No, stop it, silly— *(She shrieks with laughter, and covers her mouth so her parents won't hear.)*

JULIANNA: *(Looking in the direction of MARGARET's room)* You tucked her in, what, an hour ago?

PARIS: She's too big to get tucked in anymore, Julie.

JULIANNA: You know what I mean.

PARIS: She was sound asleep when I turned off the light.

JULIANNA: She wasn't crying again?

PARIS: I said she was under the covers, fast asleep.

MEPHISTOPHELES: You're sure, Margaret? You're sure I can't get to hell this way?

MARGARET: *(14 years old)* Positive. It says so right here. *(She opens a high school geology textbook.)* "It was the belief of Medieval man that the center of the earth was hollow, and that its very core contained a region known as Hell. Damned souls were condemned to Hell, where they labored unstini—ingly— unstintingly—" what's that mean?

MEPHISTOPHELES: It means forever.

MARGARET: "Where they labored forever until the final judgement—" you do this to me all the time. It can't mean forever, because it's only until final judgement day, see?

MEPHISTOPHELES: It means forever, Margaret.

MARGARET: Anyway, it's not hell anymore. It used to be, but it's not anymore. Now there's just molten lava, which is comprised of— *(She closes her eyes and counts on her fingers, as if remembering for a quiz.)* —igneous materials, water in a highly compressed state, and and oh, shit, it's here somewhere— *(She thumbs through the book.)*

PARIS: *(Clipping his toenails very deliberately)* You know why I think it hasn't happened yet?

JULIANNA: Why what hasn't—oh, Perry, please.

PARIS: Just because I don't talk about it all the time doesn't mean I don't think about it all the time, you know?

JULIANNA: I know. Believe me, I know.

PARIS: And I've come up with a theory.

JULIANNA: A short theory? A short theory that will let me read some more tonight?

PARIS: Yes.

JULIANNA: All right.

PARIS: See, the only way to really see another person is to stand back from them. But the only way to touch them is to—touch. And the longer two people stand there touching, the faster the distance they need to see each other disappears.
All of a sudden, they're up close and they can't see a thing.

JULIANNA: Do you think you need glasses?

PARIS: What—

JULIANNA: Glasses. Reading glasses. I'm going tomorrow. Do you want me to make an appointment?

PARIS: Julie, that's not what I was talking about at all—

JULIANNA: I know, Perry, it just made me think of it. Well, do you?

PARIS: Do you think I should?

JULIANNA: *(Shrugs)* Might as well.

MARGARET: *(Handing him the text book)*
Here it is. This proves it. It's all right here, in Chapter
One: The Creation of the World. See, it tells you
everything about the composition of the center of the
earth.

MEPHISTOPHELES: This is the nonsense they're teaching
you? This is what passes for the creation of the world?

MARGARET: It's not nonsense, it's geology.

MEPHISTOPHELES: I don't care what you call it. It is not
only incorrect, it's badly told. I hate a badly told story.
(He makes the book disappear.)

(JULIANNA is reading again.)

PARIS: But—what about my theory?

JULIANNA: Oh. That. Well, Perry, it's an interesting
theory, but I don't want to be far enough away to really
see you if means I don't get to touch you. Maybe when
we're eighty or something. Okay?

PARIS: No.

JULIANNA: I'll demonstrate the problem, Perry. If we're
too far away to touch—then— *(She puts her book down.)*
—we don't get to— *(She gives PARIS a very deep kiss.)* So.
Eighty?

PARIS: Eighty five.

MEPHISTOPHELES: Do you think you're ready to hear
the real story?

MARGARET: *(16 years old)* Oh, yes!

MEPHISTOPHELES: Well, get ready then.

*(MARGARET settles down into bed, arranges the covers
carefully.)*

MEPHISTOPHELES: Here we go.

In the beginning, God created the heavens and the earth, and Adam and Eve.

MARGARET: I know this one. Tell me another.

MEPHISTOPHELES: Adam and Eve—

MARGARET: I said I don't like this story. You hear it all the time and it's always the same.

MEPHISTOPHELES: You've never heard me tell it, have you?

MARGARET: I've heard it ever since I was a kid and it was always boooring.

MEPHISTOPHELES: The way I tell the story is different. Now listen.

Adam and Eve lived in the Garden of Eden. In all the lovely world it was the loveliest of places.

(MARGARET's *room is filled with the sounds of bird song, the wind, animals calling to each other, trees swaying in the breeze.)*

MEPHISTOPHELES: God made the Garden for them to live in because he loved them. He was both mother and father to them, and like the children they were they loved him back.

MARGARET: Doesn't sound any different to me.

MEPHISTOPHELES: Shush.

But their love for him was not enough. God had made them with another love in mind.

For while Adam and Eve loved each other, in their way, they did not love enough. At night, when the shadows fell they turned to the God who had made them, and not to each other.

MARGARET: They were frightened of the dark?

MEPHISTOPHELES: Yes, like you are.

MARGARET: I am not!

MEPHISTOPHELES: Don't interrupt. So God turned to his favorite angel, Satan, and told him to plant the loveliest of trees in a place where there was only loveliness.

(MEPHISTOPHELES *waves his hand. A magnificent tree appears.*)

MARGARET: Wow! Not bad!

JULIANNA: *(Now wearing reading glasses)* Now he's falling in love.

PARIS: Good for him.

JULIANNA: No, it's hell. When he's away from the girl he loves he's in agony. When he's with her he can't wait for the next time he'll get to be with her again. When he's with her again he starts planning to go away from her forever so that he will never have to be in agony waiting to be with her ever again.

PARIS: What?

JULIANNA: I'll tell you how it turns out.

MEPHISTOPHELES: And from this tree there came— *(He gestures. An apple appears.)* An apple. *(He picks the apple, and holds it in his hands.)* And Satan said to Eve, as God his father had commanded him to say "Bright shiny apples. Wouldn't you like one of my lovely red apples? They'll make you beautiful, they'll make you—

MARGARET: Wait a minute—that's from Snow White and the Seven Dwarves.

MEPHISTOPHELES: It is?

MARGARET: Yes.

MEPHISTOPHELES: I guess you're right. It's been so long, sometimes I forget— *(Quietly)* No, I remember what I said.

Satan said "Taste this apple. This apple which God has forbidden you. One taste and Adam will find your face as lovely to look upon as God's."

MARGARET: She tastes it.

MEPHISTOPHELES: Yes. In every story, every time.

JULIANNA: He's decided to pretend he doesn't love her so that she won't stop loving him.

PARIS: What? You're kidding.

JULIANNA: No, I think it's going to work.

PARIS: But he's been in agony because of her for three books now.

JULIANNA: He's still in agony.

PARIS: But that's a thousand pages of agony—he can't be just getting around to dumping her now.

JULIANNA: Same agony. Different girl.

MEPHISTOPHELES: Then Eve offers the apple to Adam, saying "I love you. If you would love me, taste this."

MARGARET: But Adam says no. *(18 years old)*

MEPHISTOPHELES: At first. He was afraid that if he tasted the apple he would no longer be allowed to gaze upon the face of God.
But Eve says to Adam "Your face is lovelier to look upon than His. Find me, Adam, as I have now found you."
And Adam looks at Eve, who has tasted the apple, who has disobeyed the God who loved her and who she loved.
And he knows that Eve will die.
And he tastes the apple, willing to die, unwilling to live without her.

MARGARET: He loves Eve more than he loves God, that's why.

MEPHISTOPHELES: But how, Margaret? How can he love Eve more than God? Every day, he sees God's face. Imagine what that's like. How can he give that up?

MARGARET: Well, he knows that life with Eve will be better.

MEPHISTOPHELES: How?

MARGARET: Eve knows it will be.

MEPHISTOPHELES: Yes, because she's tasted the apple. She knows what life with Adam will be like. But Adam doesn't know. He hasn't eaten of the fruit of the tree of knowledge yet. Why does he do it?

MARGARET: I don't know—tell me.

MEPHISTOPHELES: I don't know.

MARGARET: You can't end the story like that—

MEPHISTOPHELES: I didn't write the story, Margaret. I can't end it any other way.

MARGARET: But that's not fair—I bet God sends them away just like he does in all the other stories—you promised me a different story! It's not fair!! (*She starts to cry.*) God sends Satan to make them taste it, and then when they taste it, he gets angry at them and sends them away and they have to die, it's not fair.

(MEPHISTOPHELES *holds* MARGARET.)

MARGARET: Why did he plant the tree? Why did he send Satan to tempt them? He wanted them to taste the apple!

MEPHISTOPHELES: I agree.

MARGARET: So why can't he forgive them!

PARIS: (*Stops clipping his toenails, makes a little gasp*) My little toenail is disappearing.
Julie—my little toenail is almost gone!

JULIANNA: I'm reading.

PARIS: *(Grabs one of her feet and inspects her little toe)*
Yours are too—

JULIANNA: What are you talking about—

PARIS: Look—

JULIANNA: *(Quickly checks, then keeps on looking)* You're right.
You know why this is happening? It's the evolution
of man. We don't need our little toes, so they're
disappearing. Starting with the toenails.

PARIS: You really think that's all it is?

JULIANNA: Of course it is. It's probably happening
everywhere.

(JULIANNA and PARIS are both carefully inspecting their feet, horrified.)

JULIANNA: You know what my feet look like? My
mother's feet. She had the ugliest feet I ever saw. I
hated other people seeing them when we went to the
beach. I always thought it was from wearing those
spike high heels.
You know, if I put polish on my toes you wouldn't
notice it so much

PARIS: Wouldn't that just make it worse?

JULIANNA: I don't think so. Bright colors make things
bigger. It would make my little toenails look bigger.

PARIS: But that would be cheating.

JULIANNA: Yes. It would.

PARIS: My mother always used that dark red polish.

JULIANNA: Red like blood?

(PARIS nods.)

JULIANNA: Mine too.
I wonder if you can still get it.

PARIS: Funny we didn't notice this before, isn't it?

JULIANNA: It's not something you'd notice. Your feet are stuck in shoes all day.

PARIS: And they're far away—all the way down there. Now if your feet were like your hands, if you were looking at them all the time, if they were right in front of you everyday—

(JULIANNA *and* PARIS *slowly bring their hands up close, and look at them.*)

PARIS: —then you would notice that they...

(JULIANNA *and* PARIS *slowly turn their hands over, and over again.*)

JULIANNA: My mother had the most beautiful hands, when she was old.

PARIS: All the veins had worked their way up to the surface, you could see them, they were this pale deep blue, under the skin.

JULIANNA: And her skin, her skin had spotted, so that it was all different colors of light brown. Almost like gold, in places.

PARIS: Her hands were soft—so soft. Much softer, when she was old, then they had ever been.

(PARIS *takes* JULIANNA's *hands in his, and presses them to his face.*)

JULIANNA: Oh, Perry, we're old.

PARIS: No.

JULIANNA: We are. Look at my hands—they're so old—

PARIS: Shhh. Your hands are soft.

JULIANNA: Are they?

PARIS: So very soft.

MARGARET: *(20 years old. She's no longer crying.)* You have to tell me why He can't forgive them.

MEPHISTOPHELES: He was angry.

MARGARET: But he loved them.

MEPHISTOPHELES: He was angry, and maybe a little jealous, I think. He saw that they might love each other more.

MARGARET: More than they loved Him?

MEPHISTOPHELES: No, no, that would turn our little story into a soap opera. No. He was scared that they might love each other more than *He* loved *them*. That is what he couldn't forgive.

PARIS: *(Puts down the clippers, lies down)* You going to read much longer tonight?

JULIANNA: I'm almost done. All of a sudden, everyone's dead or so old that he doesn't recognize them. He goes to this party, after not seeing everyone for years, and it's like going to another planet. The world that he longed, that he lived for, is gone.

MEPHISTOPHELES: I must go now.

MARGARET: No, stay—

MEPHISTOPHELES: You know I cannot.

MARGARET: You hardly ever visit me anymore.

MEPHISTOPHELES: You're a big girl now.

MARGARET: So?

MEPHISTOPHELES: So I can't stay.

MARGARET: You can never stay and you always stay and it has nothing to do with how big I am. Are you going to sing to me this time?

MEPHISTOPHELES: Not tonight.

MARGARET: Then you'll tell me another story.

MEPHISTOPHELES: You're too big for stories, aren't you?

MARGARET: I'm not too big for anything I like.

MEPHISTOPHELES: Maybe so. But I didn't come to tell you a story. You're leaving home tomorrow for good—I came to say goodbye.

MARGARET: I'm not going into exile, you know. Thanksgiving, the Holidays—I'll be back.

MEPHISTOPHELES: I won't be.

MARGARET: I don't understand—

MEPHISTOPHELES: Neither do I, sometimes. Goodbye.

(MEPHISTOPHELES *leans over to kiss* MARGARET, *she pushes him away.*)

MARGARET: You're teasing me again, aren't you? You're just teasing me, right?

MEPHISTOPHELES: Not this time.

PARIS: *(He is lying in bed, not clipping his nails.)* Julie?

JULIANNA: *(Still reading)* What?

PARIS: *(He speaks slowly, as if he is half asleep.)* Sometimes I think—I think there's some other place—a place we could find—it's there, we just have to find it—we just have to...
I wanted you to save me from something—

JULIANNA: *(Softly, away from him)* I can't.

PARIS: From everything—

JULIANNA: *(More strongly)* I can't save you. Not from anything. Not from anything at all.

(Pause)

(JULIANNA *goes back to reading,* PARIS *goes to sleep.*)

MARGARET: I'll never see you again?

MEPHISTOPHELES: Oh, we'll see each other—but you will not remember me.

MARGARET: Of course I will.

MEPHISTOPHELES: You'd be the first one who did. *(He kisses her.)* Goodbye.

MARGARET: I'll miss you—

MEPHISTOPHELES: Sweet dreams.

MARGARET: Pleasant sleep.

(MEPHISTOPHELES holds MARGARET.)

JULIANNA: Yes. Done. *(She shuts her book joyously.)* Can you believe it, Perry, I finished a *Remembrance of Things Past*. I was beginning to think I— *(She looks over, sees he is asleep. Softy)* I finished it, Perry. *(She kisses him. She puts the book on the pile of identical black books next to the nightstand, restacks the books on top of it, takes the one that had been on the bottom on the nightstand.)* Good. Ready to start again tomorrow. *(She sees the newspaper spread out at the foot of the bed, and folds it up. She pets Sam, and discovers that he is not there. She looks around for him, gives up. She places the folded newspaper on the nightstand, and turns out the light.)*

JULIANNA: *(Softly, to PARIS)* Sweet dreams, and pleasant sleep. (She kisses him, and settles down to sleep.

(MEPHISTOPHELES leaves MARGARET's room, and slowly walks over to PARIS and JULIANNA's bed. He stands, leaning over their bed.)

PARIS: *(He wakes, looks around him, does not see MEPHISTOPHELES. He ties to go back to sleep, then sits up and turns to JULIANNA.)* Julianna? Julianna? *(He touches her, she does not wake.)* Julianna, I had a dream. We were looking down, upon a great, dark lake.
And we were falling.
Together we fell, faster and faster.

Over the face of the water.

I wanted to say to you, "Don't be afraid, it will be all right."

We came closer and closer to the dark calm water.

(He begins to cry.)

We pressed up against the great dark face of the water, faster and faster.

(He holds JULIANNA.*)* Don't be afraid, it will be all right.

(He holds her, crying.)

(Blackout)

Scene Two

*(*JULIANNA *sits on her side of the bed,* PARIS *on his.)*

MEPHISTOPHELES: Then you are ready?

*(*JULIANNA *and* PARIS *slowly stand, and walk downstage, to* MEPHISTOPHELES.*)*

PARIS: Are you sure it never—that we didn't—that it never happened?

MEPHISTOPHELES: Yes.

If it'd happened, I would have felt it.

PARIS: We tried so hard—

MEPHISTOPHELES: I know. I was here. I never left your side.

PARIS: But I know it happened—I know, it happened and you didn't see it—

MEPHISTOPHELES: It did not.

PARIS: You turned your head—you closed your eyes—

MEPHISTOPHELES: I've seen as many souls as there are stars slip through my hands.

I wanted it as much as you.

JULIANNA: Then why did you go away?

MEPHISTOPHELES: I told you—I promised you—I never left your side—

JULIANNA: He did. He went to Margaret's room.

PARIS: No—it isn't true

JULIANNA: He did. You left us.

PARIS: Maybe you made a mistake, Julie—maybe you didn't see him but he was there.

JULIANNA: We are not the one's making a mistake. He left us.

MEPHISTOPHELES: I didn't mean to—I didn't want to—I only thought I'd be gone for just a moment—I didn't think you'd miss me—I only meant to be gone for a moment—

PARIS: *(Sad)* You left us.

MEPHISTOPHELES: You slept, you watched T V, you clipped your toenails, you didn't even know I was there!

PARIS: *(Now angry as it sinks in)* You left us. You left us!

MEPHISTOPHELES: I had to—I was at your side, I never meant to leave you, and then, when it didn't happen, when it didn't happen so many, many times, I—

JULIANNA: It happened. And not once, but a hundred, a thousand times.

MEPHISTOPHELES: If it'd happened even once—I would have seen it. I would have seen the world change—I would have seen heaven dragged down to earth, where it belongs, I would have seen—

JULIANNA: It doesn't matter what you saw or didn't see!
We are together.

PARIS: And that is how you'll take us.

MEPHISTOPHELES: I cannot.

JULIANNA: You owe us that—you owe us something—

MEPHISTOPHELES: Perhaps. But you came into this world alone and that is how you'll leave it.

PARIS: Please take us together—

MEPHISTOPHELES: It can't be done. There is no union after death.

PARIS: We'll go together anyway.

MEPHISTOPHELES: If it had happened then you—
But it did not.
I'm sorry.

JULIANNA: Don't be. We'll go together. Without your help.

MEPHISTOPHELES: I had hoped, so greatly, for you both. And for myself. You came so close—I could almost feel it—I believed that you two, of all the souls on earth—
(Almost whispering to himself)
It's against the rules. It's never been done. But for you, I'll do it. Yes, I'll do it. *(Triumphantly)*
You can have another chance. Another lifetime of chances. It doesn't have to end like this—I have the power, all it takes is a little courage—I can turn the clock back, give you back your youth, we'll start all over, we'll try again.

PARIS: What?

MEPHISTOPHELES: Yes! Of course! This next time, there's no question, of course it will happen.

JULIANNA: *(Laughing)* You make me laugh. Don't you know what it was like, at all? You say you were here—I don't think you were really here for an instant.
To be young again—when I was young that would have seemed like paradise itself. You want to live

forever when you're young. Then you grow old, and
you forget what living forever was supposed to be like.
Why should I want to be young again? All these years
I've had with Paris beside me would be gone.

PARIS: You're telling us that what we had was not
enough.
You have no right to tell us that.

MEPHISTOPHELES: You can have a chance for more—

PARIS: And Margaret, what about her? Does she just
vanish, in a puff of smoke? *(Angry)* Our life is ours!
You cannot take that away. *(He takes JULIANNA's hand.)*
Enough.

JULIANNA: Enough.

PARIS: When will it happen?

MEPHISTOPHELES: I may not say.

JULIANNA: You won't try to stop us from going
together?

MEPHISTOPHELES: You are no longer mine.

PARIS: And our souls?

MEPHISTOPHELES: Are yours.
For now.

PARIS: Then leave us. Leave us alone together.

MEPHISTOPHELES: I'll miss you both, I'll—

*(JULIANNA and PARIS do not notice him any longer. They
walk hand in hand downstage.)*

PARIS: What do you think it will be like?

JULIANNA: I don't know.

PARIS: Do you think there's a heaven?

JULIANNA: I know there's one, with you.

PARIS: It will be harder for Margaret this way.

JULIANNA: Both of us, you mean, at once?

PARIS: Maybe one of us should—

JULIANNA: Oh Perry, I don't know.

PARIS: Julianna—

JULIANNA: Don't make me stay without you. Please—I couldn't—

PARIS: You think I could better than you?

JULIANNA: I couldn't—I can't—

PARIS: Then I will.

JULIANNA: No—I won't let you—I love you too much—

PARIS: Enough, Julianna. Let me stay. Let me be the one who stays. Not for long.

JULIANNA: I can't—

PARIS: What will I be when you leave me? An old man who loves you. I'm that already. Believe me. There will be many times, before I join you, when I will be sure that you are still with me here. I wonder what that will be like. To lie in bed without you beside me. I'm sure I will be quite afraid, at first.

(PARIS *walks along the stage, leaving* JULIANNA *in a pool of light.*)

PARIS: And Sam won't be there, thumping away. I wonder why it never seemed strange to us that a poodle could live for fifty or sixty years. Yes, it will be very frightening at first. Then I suppose it will just be very sad.

(*The light on* JULIANNA *begins to fade.*)

PARIS: I don't suppose I can tell Margaret about all this. She's a very practical girl, your daughter. Takes after you in so many ways. When I look at her I sometimes see the moment when I met you.

Sometimes I think that was the moment we were
searching for all along.

You meet someone who makes you believe in all the
things you want to believe in. There's really nothing
like that. It makes you do crazy things. You look at
them—and what, after all, are they—eyes and hair,
nose and mouth—mostly just a lot of air and water,
really. But you see something magnificent in all that.
When I first saw you, I recognized something that I
thought I had forgotten. I can't quite remember what
it was, now, but I know it's there. I see it sometimes
when I look at Margaret. Yes, that's the moment I see
when I look at her.

Julianna, I—

(PARIS *turns to* JULIANNA. *He sees the moment when she
disappears.*)

(*There is a harsh, terrible sound. A flash of light*)

(*Blackout*)

(*Lights up on* MARGARET, *walking into her apartment.
She is unaware that a large black cocker spaniel, wearing
a studded red collar and walking with a slight limp, has
followed her into the room.*)

(*Blackout*)

END OF PLAY

www.ingramcontent.com/pod-product-compliance
Lightning Source LLC
Chambersburg PA
CBHW070023110426
42741CB00034B/2418